# TAURUS

# HOROSCOPE

# & ASTROLOGY

# 2022

Published by Mystic Cat Press

Suite SM-2380-6403

14601 North Bybee Lake Court

Portland, Oregon 97203

Phone: +1 (805) 308-6503

SiaSands@hotmail.com

# Contents

# TAURUS 2022
# HOROSCOPE & ASTROLOGY

Four Weeks Per Month

Week 1 – Days 1 - 7

Week 2 – Days 8 - 14

Week 3 – Days 15 - 21

Week 4 – Days 22 – Month-end

# Taurus

**Taurus Dates:** April 20th to May 20th

**Zodiac Symbol:** Bull

**Element:** Earth

**Planet:** Venus

**House:** Second

**Color:** Green

# 2022 AT A GLANCE

## Eclipses

Partial Solar – April 30th

Total Lunar – May 16th

Partial Solar – October 25th

Total Lunar -November 8th

## Equinoxes and Solstices

Spring - March 20th

Summer - June 21st

Fall – September 23rd

Winter – December 21st

## Mercury Retrogrades

January 14th, Aquarius - February 4th Capricorn

May 10th, Gemini - June 3rd, Taurus

September 10th, Libra - October 2nd Virgo

December 29th, Capricorn - January 1st, 2023, Capricorn

# 2022 FULL MOONS

Wolf Moon: January 17th, 23:48.

Snow Moon: February 16th, 16:57

Worm Moon March 18th, 07:17

Pink Moon: April 16th, 18:54

Flower Moon: May 16th, 04:13

Strawberry Moon: June 14th, 11:51

Buck Moon: July 13th, 18:37

Sturgeon Moon: August 12th, 01:35

Corn, Harvest Moon: September 10th, 09:59

Hunters Moon: October 9th, 20:54

Beaver Moon: November 8th, 11:01

Cold Moon: December 8th, 04:07

# THE MOON PHASES

◉ New Moon (Dark Moon)

◉ Waxing Crescent Moon

◉ First Quarter Moon

◉ Waxing Gibbous Moon

◉ Full Moon

◉ Waning Gibbous (Disseminating) Moon

◉ Third (Last/Reconciling) Quarter Moon

◉ Waning Crescent (Balsamic) Moon

# 2022

## JANUARY
| M | T | W | T | F | S | S |
|---|---|---|---|---|---|---|
|   |   |   |   |   | 1 | 2 |
| 3 | 4 | 5 | 6 | 7 | 8 | 9 |
| 10 | 11 | 12 | 13 | 14 | 15 | 16 |
| 17 | 18 | 19 | 20 | 21 | 22 | 23 |
| 24 | 25 | 26 | 27 | 28 | 29 | 30 |
| 31 |   |   |   |   |   |   |

## FEBRUARY
| M | T | W | T | F | S | S |
|---|---|---|---|---|---|---|
|   | 1 | 2 | 3 | 4 | 5 | 6 |
| 9 | 10 | 11 | 12 | 11 | 12 | 13 |
| 14 | 15 | 16 | 17 | 18 | 19 | 20 |
| 21 | 22 | 23 | 24 | 25 | 26 | 27 |
| 28 |   |   |   |   |   |   |

## MARCH
| M | T | W | T | F | S | S |
|---|---|---|---|---|---|---|
|   | 1 | 2 | 3 | 4 | 4 | 6 |
| 7 | 8 | 9 | 10 | 11 | 12 | 13 |
| 14 | 15 | 16 | 17 | 18 | 19 | 20 |
| 21 | 22 | 23 | 24 | 25 | 26 | 27 |
| 28 | 29 | 30 | 31 |   |   |   |

## APRIL
| M | T | W | T | F | S | S |
|---|---|---|---|---|---|---|
|   |   |   |   | 1 | 2 | 3 |
| 4 | 5 | 6 | 7 | 8 | 9 | 10 |
| 11 | 12 | 13 | 14 | 15 | 16 | 17 |
| 18 | 19 | 20 | 21 | 22 | 23 | 24 |
| 25 | 26 | 27 | 28 | 29 | 30 |   |

## MAY
| M | T | W | T | F | S | S |
|---|---|---|---|---|---|---|
|   |   |   |   |   |   | 1 |
| 2 | 3 | 4 | 5 | 6 | 7 | 8 |
| 9 | 10 | 11 | 12 | 13 | 14 | 15 |
| 16 | 17 | 18 | 19 | 20 | 21 | 22 |
| 23 | 24 | 25 | 26 | 27 | 28 | 29 |
| 30 | 31 |   |   |   |   |   |

## JUNE
| M | T | W | T | F | S | S |
|---|---|---|---|---|---|---|
|   | 1 | 2 | 3 | 4 | 5 |   |
| 6 | 7 | 8 | 9 | 10 | 11 | 12 |
| 13 | 14 | 15 | 16 | 17 | 18 | 19 |
| 20 | 21 | 22 | 23 | 24 | 25 | 26 |
| 27 | 28 | 29 | 30 |   |   |   |

## JULY
| M | T | W | T | F | S | S |
|---|---|---|---|---|---|---|
|   |   |   |   | 1 | 2 | 3 |
| 4 | 5 | 6 | 7 | 8 | 9 | 10 |
| 11 | 12 | 13 | 14 | 15 | 16 | 17 |
| 18 | 19 | 20 | 21 | 22 | 23 | 24 |
| 25 | 26 | 27 | 28 | 29 | 30 | 31 |

## AUGUST
| M | T | W | T | F | S | S |
|---|---|---|---|---|---|---|
| 1 | 2 | 3 | 4 | 5 | 6 | 7 |
| 8 | 9 | 10 | 11 | 12 | 13 | 14 |
| 15 | 16 | 17 | 18 | 19 | 20 | 21 |
| 22 | 23 | 24 | 25 | 26 | 27 | 28 |
| 29 | 30 | 31 |   |   |   |   |

## SEPTEMBER
| M | T | W | T | F | S | S |
|---|---|---|---|---|---|---|
|   |   |   | 1 | 2 | 3 | 4 |
| 5 | 6 | 7 | 8 | 9 | 10 | 11 |
| 12 | 13 | 14 | 15 | 16 | 17 | 18 |
| 19 | 20 | 21 | 22 | 23 | 24 | 25 |
| 26 | 27 | 28 | 29 | 30 |   |   |

## OCTOBER
| M | T | W | T | F | S | S |
|---|---|---|---|---|---|---|
|   |   |   |   |   | 1 | 2 |
| 3 | 4 | 5 | 6 | 7 | 8 | 9 |
| 10 | 11 | 12 | 13 | 14 | 15 | 16 |
| 17 | 18 | 19 | 20 | 21 | 22 | 23 |
| 24 | 25 | 26 | 27 | 28 | 29 | 30 |
| 31 |   |   |   |   |   |   |

## NOVEMBER
| M | T | W | T | F | S | S |
|---|---|---|---|---|---|---|
|   | 1 | 2 | 3 | 4 | 5 | 6 |
| 7 | 8 | 9 | 10 | 11 | 12 | 13 |
| 14 | 15 | 16 | 17 | 18 | 19 | 20 |
| 21 | 22 | 23 | 24 | 25 | 26 | 27 |
| 28 | 29 | 30 |   |   |   |   |

## DECEMBER
| M | T | W | T | F | S | S |
|---|---|---|---|---|---|---|
|   |   |   | 1 | 2 | 3 | 4 |
| 5 | 6 | 7 | 8 | 9 | 10 | 11 |
| 12 | 13 | 14 | 15 | 16 | 17 | 18 |
| 19 | 20 | 21 | 22 | 23 | 24 | 25 |
| 26 | 27 | 28 | 29 | 30 | 31 |   |

Time set to Coordinated Universal Time Zone

(UT±0)


Meteor Showers are on the date they peak.

# JANUARY

| Sun | Mon | Tue | Wed | Thu | Fri | Sat |
|-----|-----|-----|-----|-----|-----|-----|
|     |     |     |     |     |     | 1   |
| 2   | 3   | 4   | 5   | 6   | 7   | 8   |
| 9   | 10  | 11  | 12  | 13  | 14  | 15  |
| 16  | 17  | 18  | 19  | 20  | 21  | 22  |
| 23  | 24  | 25  | 26  | 27  | 28  | 29  |
| 30  | 31  |     |     |     |     |     |

January 2nd - New Moon in Capricorn 18:33

January 3rd - Quadrantids Meteor Shower. January 1$^{st}$-5$^{th}$.

January 7th - Mercury at Greatest Eastern Elongation

January 9th - First Quarter Moon in Aries 18:11

January 14th - Mercury Retrograde begins in Aquarius

January 17th - Wolf Moon. Full Moon in Cancer 23:48

January 25th - Last Quarter Moon Scorpio 13:42

# NEW MOON

# FULL MOON

The Quadrantids Meteor Shower blazes across the night sky this week. It marks a time of rejuvenation that offers room to grow your life. The rough edges diminish, and that sweeps away areas that are no longer relevant. You herald a busy time that helps you move forward towards new adventures. Good fortune arrives that has you thinking big about future goals. It underscores the energy of abundance and manifestation at your disposal. Building the right foundation draws dividends.

Things are on the move for your life soon. It does highlight a path forward that brings growth. You have the time and motivation to focus on advancing goals. It sets in motion the essence of manifestation that gently shifts your focus towards a long term destination. Creative energy brews up a storm of potential that ushers in change. Metamorphosis is occurring that cracks the code to a new path. It draws renewal, rejuvenation, and healing. It elevates potential and kicks the cobwebs to the curb.

You are in the process of creating change. It helps you move forward towards developing a cherished dream. It does bring a chance to network and get involved with your social life. You scoop the pool and discover a journey that ushers in new potential. It brings a clear path that lets you dive in and embrace advancing your world. News arrives that gets a boost; this information offers a nugget of gold for your personal life.

Mercury Retrograde begins in Aquarius at the week's end. Being mindful and consciously walking a lighter path throughout this retrograde phase removes the tension. It creates space to cultivate your interests. It may feel like a slowdown or lack of progress, but in reality, it's a valuable time to check in with your intuition and explore options that speak to your heart. An endeavor ahead brings the development of a project that inspires your mind; it has you investing your energy wisely in a resourceful area.

It is a time of rapid growth that teaches you the value of resilience. You navigate a complex environment and come out a winner. It lets you set sail on a timely voyage of improving your circumstances. A gateway ahead brings a journey of excitement and adventure. It is a time of waiting for new information. It lets you touch down in a more abundant landscape. News arrives to get the ball rolling forward.

You face a crossroads, and this brings change. It does draw a reflective and introspective chapter as you contemplate the path ahead. You make a decision that brings a turning point. It liberates the tension and attracts abundance and social support. It does trigger a new chapter for your social life that draws the opportunity to nurture a bond. It brings a path that tempts you forward and enriches your life.

The Wolf Moon. Full Moon in Cancer this week sees you working smarter and conserving resources by focusing on the most critical areas. Prioritizing the path forward brings efficiency and opportunities for growth. It draws stability and improves your bottom line. There is a chance to learn new skills; your willingness to be open to all possibilities draws innovative options. It is a good time to trust your instincts and broaden your scope. An excellent bonus crop up that brings a boost. It does seem a new role is on offer soon, and this brings growth.

Life becomes a whirlwind in the most delicious manner. It brings a piece of welcome news. It helps you cut away from areas that limit progress and are no longer relevant. Distancing yourself from drama removes stress and tension. It helps you build stable foundations from which to grow your world. Clearing the decks offers a chance to immerse yourself in a new area. Nurturing your environment removes the blocks and provides a path that brings prosperity into focus. It provides you with an enterprising approach forward. Your pioneering attitude blazes the way towards a dynamic and active environment.

It shows your circumstances improving. Taking time to re-evaluate progress, being open to new possibilities supports a chapter of personal growth. It brings a journey that expands into new areas and offers the chance to advance your skills.

The past has been a time of overcoming challenges, learning the ropes in unfamiliar environments, and a great time of personal growth. It has let you make strides in developing your life. It's has taught you value and meaning, enabling you to be discerning and set the bar higher. Nurturing your environment brings a focus that helps heal the wounded parts of your spirit. An aspect of the past may impact you, and creating space to unpack memories draws acceptance, which lifts the burden. Positive influences soon flow into your world.

It is a time of change, and this brings an awakening. It lets you make a breakthrough regarding your career path. Planning this journey has you thinking about the future in a new light. You open a fresh book chapter, and progression shines radiantly on the horizon. It does connect you with a successful individual who helps improve your prospects. Remaining committed, focused, and proactively brings rewards.

News arrives soon that unpacks a favorable chapter. It brings an additional project that captures your interest. It does get research, collaboration, and support. Shifting your attention to a compelling journey forward draws dividends. It brings a social aspect that connects you with friends and acquaintances. Sharing thoughts and ideas yield a bumper crop of potential.

# FEBRUARY

| Sun | Mon | Tue | Wed | Thu | Fri | Sat |
|-----|-----|-----|-----|-----|-----|-----|
|     |     | 1   | 2   | 3   | 4   | 5   |
| 6   | 7   | 8   | 9   | 10  | 11  | 12  |
| 13  | 14  | 15  | 16  | 17  | 18  | 19  |
| 20  | 21  | 22  | 23  | 24  | 25  | 26  |
| 27  | 28  |     |     |     |     |     |

February 1st - New Moon in Aquarius 05:45
February 1st - Chinese New Year (Tiger)
February 1st - Imbolc

February 4th - Mercury Retrograde ends in Capricorn

February 8th - First Quarter Moon in Taurus 13:50

February 16th - Mercury at Greatest Western Elongation
February 16th - Snow Moon. Full Moon in Leo 16:57

February 23rd - Last Quarter Moon in Scorpio 22:32

# NEW MOON

# FULL MOON

Advancement is brewing in your life's background; it does create a potent mix that captures the essence of creativity to blend ideas with tangible results. New options arrive that inspire your mind. A project gets the go-ahead, new ideas, and inspiration to flow into your world. It does help you progress a dream vision. It begins a trend of improving your circumstances and advancing your fortune forward. You begin to see impressive growth is possible when you think beyond the box. A successful person reaches out to encourage you and cultivate a close friendship.

Focusing on the essentials lets, you make the right move towards a lofty goal. It helps you establish your talents in an area ripe for progression. Understanding your vision and tuning into your passions does open the gateway forward. It moves you in alignment with your spirit, and you can look forward to a refreshing and lively change of pace.

Sudden changes can feel unsettling but ultimately take you towards transformation. You can untangle challenges and head towards your vision. Expanding the boundaries of your life draws happiness and rewarding outcomes. Luck and opportunity greet you on this curious path. New possibilities flood your life with potential, which see you doing well, keeping busy with adventures and passion projects.

There is an improvement coming around home and family life. It is a busy time that brings an end to disappointment. It offers new adventures that inspire and delight. It brings a highly social environment that connects you with a crew of innovative characters. You invest your energy in a situation that offers room to progress. It does bring a time of heightened creativity and enterprising options. You enter a growth cycle that takes your vision to a new level.

It is a time where you see improvement flowing into your world. It brings a social patch that connects you with someone who inspires your mind. It brings happy developments as life moves forward towards new opportunities. Nurturing your social life draws dividends. It gets personal growth and takes you towards an environment that is expressive, joyful, and abundant. Building stable foundations plant the right seeds.

Singles may discover that an introduction paves the way forward for your social life. It brings a unique situation into focus. It marks a time that brings confidence, which lets you push back the barriers and open your life. It brings inspiring conversations and a fanciful aspect that has you thinking about the possibilities. It sets the tone for a happy chapter that nurtures your life.

The Full Moon in Leo this week does wipe the slate clean on many levels. You get the go-ahead to expand your life. It migrates away from troubles and brings a breezy influence into your world. You are ready to set sail on a voyage that brings happiness and abundance to your life. It does get a time that places the spotlight on achieving your vision. Constructive dialogues with friends bring a new possibility to light. It introduces you to someone who plays an integral part in future events. Changes swirl around your social life. Little goes under your radar as you focus on achieving your dreams. You are the captain of your ship. You come from a long line of trailblazers and should invest in your talents. Using your abilities brings goodness to the top. Something new and tempting arrives, and it brings a breakthrough. It is a breath of fresh air that renews your energy, drawing rejuvenation. It takes you towards an expansive and happy chapter. It is music for your soul. You are currently transitioning to a potent phase of heightened opportunity. Climbing the pinnacle of success lets you appreciate how diverse and broad your journey has been.

You can giddy-up and charge into a new area. Indeed, contemplating options sparks and heightens your creativity. It gets the ball rolling by setting intentions to improve your circumstances. Your imagination paves the way forward. It draws rejuvenation and lets you rewrite the rules. You can create magic; confidence is on the rise and leading the way towards a new endeavor.

New possibilities light a fire under your inspiration soon. It brings stable foundations, and this lets you navigate an uncertain time with relative ease. You make good progress on developing a goal. It sparks a journey that offers pearls of wisdom. It does have you feeling optimistic about the prospects ahead. The wayside flings limitations aside as you enter this transformational chapter of growth.

It does seem like the perfect vantage spot from which to grow your world. It lights a path of inspiration and creativity; it has you expanding your options into new areas. It does bring a time of increasing your abilities and putting the shine on talents. Having a stable basis from which to expand your world becomes a vital step towards a brighter future. It does build grounded foundations that nurture wellness and harmony.

There is plenty of excitement ahead when you land a prime-time role. It does see you diverging from your everyday routine. New responsibilities and options inspire growth. It does see you working with your skills and refining your abilities. Don't be afraid to extend your reach into new areas. It is a valuable tool that grows your abilities. Putting the shine on your talents gets your work noticed. It does bring recognition, and it offers a chance to fully develop your abilities in a new area.

# MARCH

| Sun | Mon | Tue | Wed | Thu | Fri | Sat |
|-----|-----|-----|-----|-----|-----|-----|
|     |     | 1   | 2   | 3   | 4   | 5   |
| 6   | 7   | 8   | 9   | 10  | 11  | 12  |
| 13  | 14  | 15  | 16  | 17  | 18  | 19  |
| 20  | 21  | 22  | 23  | 24  | 25  | 26  |
| 27  | 28  | 29  | 30  | 31  |     |     |

March 2nd - New Moon in Pisces 17:34

March 10th - First Quarter Moon in Gemini 10:45

March 18th - Worm Moon. Full Moon in Virgo 07:17

March 20th - Ostara/Spring Equinox 15:33

March 25th - Last Quarter Moon in Capricorn 05:37

# NEW MOON

# FULL MOON

New Moon in Pisces reveals a new undercurrent of potential that surrounds your life. A window of opportunity opens; this offers a gateway towards a happy chapter. It brings an innovative time that blazes a trail towards your chosen vision. Stumbling blocks get kicked out of the path; your focus is determined and confident. Raising the bar elevates your situation; it is instrumental in helping you discover a new area that increases your knowledge and wisdom.

There are many routes to your chosen destination. As one door closes, you soon discover another path forward. Finding suitable workarounds makes the best use of your creativity. It elevates potential and offers valuable rewards. It is a time to shine and discover the opportunities that shift you forward. It brings a busy time that enables you to develop a venture with friends.

You spotlight an avenue that offers fruitful results. It does let you unpack a new chapter and begin developing a goal that provides room to progress into a passion project. Improvement flows into your world and brings a fresh perspective. It lets you connect with like-minded individuals who offer enterprising thoughts and lively discussions. It is an ideal time for directing your energy towards developing goals.

It's a great time to map out goals. A willingness to explore new possibilities opens a unique road. Intuition and creativity flow into your world to assist a journey forward. There are developments around your life that bring the building blocks of stability. The time is ripe to progress your vision and align your thoughts towards future possibilities. Prioritizing goals streamlines the path; it captures the essence of efficiency.

Life lights up with new possibilities. It encourages a shift forward. Focusing on developing the path rules a time of sunny skies. It does bring sunshine after rain. All systems point to a smoother ride and a happier chapter ahead. If you have felt life's struggles weighing you down, you can lift the lid on an enterprising chapter that inspires and grows your world.

As your thoughts turn to the past, a sentimental vibe cloaks your energy in treasured memories. It does have you traversing the decades and unpacking ideas and wisdom that provide insight and clarity into your life. It puts you in touch with deep emotions, and this draws a gateway of healing energy. It underscores an atmosphere of personal growth that puts you on the path towards a higher calling. A focus on freedom and expansion rejuvenates your spirit and brings a new way forward into focus. It does reveal a journey ripe for development as you continue the evolution of self.

Full Moon in Virgo this week. At the end of the week, Ostara/Spring Equinox brings the Sun again after the long winter. Life offers the chance to follow your vision soon. You have more control over the road ahead than you may currently understand. A new start flows into your life; plenty of activity afoot shines a light on a productive growth phase. It creates a strong basis from which to journey forward. It has you feeling inspired and ready to take on new responsibilities with enthusiasm.

This self-discovery time enables profound personal growth. Your willingness to unearth new areas plays an important part in relieving the stress and tension in your life. It sweeps away outworn energy and lets you walk a path that dazzles with possibilities. It leads to a productive and enterprising chapter. New adventures tempt you forward towards an exciting landscape.

Focusing on the basics takes you to the building blocks of life. As you peel back the layers, you reveal the refreshing potential that expands your situation. It revolutionizes your environment and draws enthusiasm. Positive changes are looming that see more energy flowing into your world; being willing and open to change advances your trajectory. It brings a journey of discovery that is adventurous and inspiring. A social path blossoms under a productive sky. It is a time that nurtures well-being as it draws new possibilities into your world.

Focusing on priorities brings a diligent and active time. Driving your energy in a focused manner lets you achieve growth. It marks a significant time where change is possible. You are supported to reach for your dreams and develop your goals. Exciting visions of a future destination guides this process, letting you dream big and go for a pinnacle. You meet someone edgy and outspoken; this person becomes a guide and mentor who assists this growth and learning journey. Refining your talents sharpens your skills; it shines a light on new possibilities.

You're on a continuous cycle of growth and change. It does let you explore learning new areas. Advancing your abilities brings a boost. You are ready to lift the lid on your potential. Broadening your horizons brings an uplifting time of focusing on a passion project. It shines a light on lively discussions and group bonding sessions. If you have been feeling sidetracked recently, you soon get back on course and focus on progressing your goals. It's a time that reinvents and elevates the potential possible in your world.

It brings an improvement of stability to your home front. A compelling journey awaits your open heart and mind. It helps you release your troubles, and it reconnects you to what is most endearing. It brings an enriching time of developing the path ahead. An area you focus on gets the green light to move forward, and you can appreciate a lucky break.

# APRIL

| Sun | Mon | Tue | Wed | Thu | Fri | Sat |
|-----|-----|-----|-----|-----|-----|-----|
|     |     |     |     |     | 1   | 2   |
| 3   | 4   | 5   | 6   | 7   | 8   | 9   |
| 10  | 11  | 12  | 13  | 14  | 15  | 16  |
| 17  | 18  | 19  | 20  | 21  | 22  | 23  |
| 24  | 25  | 26  | 27  | 28  | 29  | 30  |

April 1st - New Moon in Aries 06:24

April 9th - First Quarter Moon in Cancer 06:47

April 16th - Pink Moon. Full Moon in Libra 18:54

April 22nd - Lyrids Meteor Shower from April 16-25

April 23rd - Last Quarter Moon in Aquarius 11:56.

April 29th - Mercury Greatest Eastern Elongation of 20.6 degrees from the Sun.

April 30th - New Moon in Taurus 20:27

# NEW MOON

# FULL MOON

New Moon in Aries this week lets you reach a crossroads that brings new options, and it encourages decisive action. It brings the opportunity to develop the road ahead proactively. You discover an opening that speaks volumes about the person you are becoming. It does see you merge dreams with aspirations and dive into uncharted territory. It's an empowering chapter that lets you dig deep and reveal the truth of what your higher calling involves. It's a time of self-discovery and resolving issues that hold you back from achieving your vision. Prioritizing and streamlining the path ahead is a dramatic tool that cuts await procrastination. It brings an enterprising chapter that builds new skills. Methodically laying the groundwork paves the way forward.

You enter the high energy and social chapter that brings engagement and support. A community endeavor opens the floodgates to a happier chapter. Fires of creativity burn brightly, drawing innovative solutions and new enterprises. Being open to change brings impressive results. It emphasizes a time of developing bonds that offer room to grow your social life. It brings opportunities to unwind with friends and kindred spirits. You find your sense of balance and embrace developing the path ahead. Generating leads brings new possibilities to light the way forward.

Now is the perfect time to develop goals that have been on the backburner. It does bring learning and growth that inspires change. Capturing the essence of an abundant mindset draws well-being into your world. A shift of perception redirects your attention to an area that offers gold. Setting intentions provides a mix of manifestation that is essential in cracking the path wide open.

Advancement is coming into your life soon. It is an upgrade that arrives out of the blue and opens the path ahead to progress your career. It rules a time of expansion and progress. You resolve restrictions and crack the code to future ambitions. Advancement is looming, and this takes you to a diligent time of building your vision. It takes your abilities to the next level and ignites a substantial phase of growth.

A blended approach with another person initiates a new beginning. It offers progression and brings inspiration flowing into your world. It marks the start of a productive chapter that lets you chase your passion. It marks a new beginning when an ample opportunity tempts you forward. You negotiate a dazzling path that glimmers with possibilities. Communication arrives to get the ball rolling.

The Full Moon in Libra illuminates that you have an incredible ability to stay true to your heart and vision. It does see you moving in alignment with your spirit. Nurturing creativity offers dividends. It brings new possibilities, and this opens the path forward. Revamping your trajectory lets you progress your life and avoid repeating old patterns of behavior. Making your vision a priority is essential in achieving the kind of growth you seek.

Events align to form a favorable window of opportunity. It shines a light on a chapter of rejuvenation that refreshes your spirit and brings renewal to your world. Turning your attention to the home front improves foundations. You thrive in an environment of increasing security. Life picks up steam, and this increases overall enthusiasm and energy. As your motivation sparks brightly, an influx of creativity brings a new venture to mind.

It is a time that rules endings, and this lets you achieve closure—healing the past acts as a catalyst for change. You glide into the new potential that enables you to get involved with developing your life. It reawakens creativity as you exploring an interest that inspires growth. It gifts you the wind beneath your wings. As inspiration comes flooding into your world, you discover you can sidestep hurdles and overcome barriers.

Lyrids Meteor Shower brings a powerhouse of fresh energy into your environment. Lovely changes flow into your life, and this gets a chance to develop goals. Your creativity heightens, bringing refreshing ideas and insights into the path ahead. Your willingness to explore new areas plays a vital role in unearthing hidden gems of potential. It puts you in charge of proactively nurturing your environment and harnessing the power of manifestation to advance life forward.

Mercury's Greatest Eastern Elongation can feel disquieting. Still, you have energy that strengthens your spirit and elevates your potential more than you currently realize. As you expand your life, you double up on creativity and stir up new goals to light the way forward. Life is changing; you benefit from being flexible and adaptable. It is a significant time for self-discovery and growth. You connect with others who join you to ushers in new energy and fresh possibilities. You land in an environment ripe for growing your dreams.

The future is looking brighter all the time. Life turns the corner and heads to an upswing. It brings an optimistic phase of developing goals. You reach a turning point, and this pushes back barriers. It unleashes your abilities in an area ripe for advancement. It brings an entrepreneurial aspect that harnesses creativity to great benefit. It shines a light on learning a new skill. It motivates you to dig deep and unearth the next step forward.

# MAY

| Sun | Mon | Tue | Wed | Thu | Fri | Sat |
|-----|-----|-----|-----|-----|-----|-----|
| 1 | 2 | 3 | 4 | 5 | 6 | 7 |
| 8 | 9 | 10 | 11 | 12 | 13 | 14 |
| 15 | 16 | 17 | 18 | 19 | 20 | 21 |
| 22 | 23 | 24 | 25 | 26 | 27 | 28 |
| 29 | 30 | 31 | | | | |

May 6th - Eta Aquarids Meteor Shower, April 19th - May 28th

May 9th - First Quarter Moon in Leo 00:21

May 10th - Mercury Retrograde begins in Gemini

May 16th - Total Lunar Eclipse 01:32

May 16th - Flower Moon. Full Moon in Scorpio 04:13

May 22nd - Last Quarter Moon in Aquarius 18:43

May - 30th - New Quarter Moon in Leo 00:21

# NEW MOON

# FULL MOON

Eta Aquarids Meteor Shower brings an opportunity to broaden your vision; it brings a time of expansion, freedom, and optimism. A positive chapter head highlights improvement. It comes just in the nick of time to get a boost of abundance into your world. It fans the fires of inspiration and opens a favorable chapter that lets you take steps towards developing an interest that inspires your mind. It has you busy planning for future contingencies and connecting with others on a similar wavelength.

A long-forgotten dream is ready to make a grand entrance. As you stand on the precipice of change, you discover an open path towards your vision. It brings the music into your life; it does highlight developing goals. The fires of inspiration burn brightly, allowing progress to guide the path ahead. You feel in sync with other kindred spirits, and this draws a valuable sense of connection.

Life heats up with new potential soon. An invitation and lengthy conversations see your social life turns the corner and head to a happy chapter. There is support swirling around your life, giving you the green light to network and connect with friends. It brings lighter energy and the chance to mingle with people who understand you on a deeper level. It's prime time to set aspirations and plan goals. New inspiration and people enter into your life for good reason in the coming chapter.

Mercury Retrograde begins in Gemini. Removing the drama by placing appropriate barriers clears the path ahead. Perseverance and determination help you juggle life and maintain various projects while keeping your eye on new possibilities. If you feel stuck or restricted, remember to get those balls in the air and start shifting your energy forward. Setting aspirations and goals activate your power and primes your creativity. It brings new ideas that help cut away from areas that didn't bear fruit.

A focus on rebuilding foundations brings stability and balance. It leads to a busy time that sees headway occurring around larger goals. It triggers a stable phase of growth that sets the right tone to help things come together with intention. It does smooth out the road's bumps and lets the journey progress towards a more abundant landscape. There is an opportunity ahead that brings a gateway towards a happier phase.

Your ability to navigate life's ups and downs helps you make the most of the future potential. Waves of possibility tempt you towards growth. As you set sail on your ship of dreams, you discover purpose stands beside you. It does bring a driven time that gets the ball rolling on a new phase of growth. It helps you accomplish a great deal, and it sparks new options for social connection and friendship.

Communicating more with your friends helps nurture wellness, and this attracts a new phase. Lighter energy flows into your situation, bringing more insight into the path ahead. It does help you walk away from stormy weather and feel more comfortable about prospects. The course ahead clears, and sunny skies re-emerge overhead. It brings solutions; it unleashes creativity, and this gets the magic flowing freely in your world.

The more you offer your gifts to the broader world's potential, the more you surround yourself with abundance and possibility. It does break down barriers and open the path ahead. Cultivating your desires on a deeper level merges with an aspect of manifestation and helps you achieve your vision. It brings a unique journey that offers room to grow your goals. Travel, exploration, and freedom help you live your most wild adventures.

It's time to map out your goals. Be untamed, live your most wild dreams. It's about getting back to what you seek and not becoming distracted by the conditions around you. It takes community, support, and creativity to nurture your spirit. The more you own the path ahead, the more you attract like-minded people into your sphere. Being true to yourself lets you step into full alignment with the person you are becoming. It underscores how instrumental it is to be open to change and to remain flexible to new opportunities. Shedding the layers that hold you back clears the air; it renews and rejuvenates by releasing outworn areas.

The increased potential around home life brings a breath of fresh air into your surrounding that is appreciated. It brings grounded energy that restores balance. Your ideas and vision for the future gain traction. As the momentum picks up pace, you focus energy on developing an enterprising journey forward. Changes sweep in that encourage growth; you reach a fork in the road where your heart leads towards purpose and potential. An area you invest your time in developing draws a positive outcome. It draws stability and heightens the security in your world. It is a journey that offers abundance, transformation, and growth. Something is on offer that elevates your role to a new level. It brings a chapter that gives you something to celebrate. Productive dialogues draw open communication; this is vital and productive. It helps you focus your energy on an area that offers substantial growth.

The tides are turning in your favor. The new potential is on the horizon; it reveals a positive shift forward. You reap the rewards and embrace mapping out new possibilities. Information arrives soon that stirs up new potential. It gives you a chance to build strong foundations. It does bring a transition that helps you break through to a lucky chapter. It draws more stability into your world, and this heightens the sense of well-being and harmony. You are ready to nurture a new area; as you direct your energy towards growing your world, you discover an opportunity to learn and prosper.

# JUNE

| Sun | Mon | Tue | Wed | Thu | Fri | Sat |
|-----|-----|-----|-----|-----|-----|-----|
|     |     |     | 1   | 2   | 3   | 4   |
| 5   | 6   | 7   | 8   | 9   | 10  | 11  |
| 12  | 13  | 14  | 15  | 16  | 17  | 18  |
| 19  | 20  | 21  | 22  | 23  | 24  | 25  |
| 26  | 27  | 28  | 29  | 30  |     |     |

# ASTROLOGY

June 3rd - Mercury Retrograde ends in Taurus

June 7th - First Quarter Moon in Virgo 14:48

June 14th - Strawberry Moon. Full Moon in Sagittarius Supermoon 11:51

June 16th - Mercury's greatest Western elongation of 23.2 degrees from the Sun

June 21st - Last Quarter Moon in Aries 03:11

June 21st - Midsummer/Litha Solstice 09:13

June 29th - New Moon in Cancer 02:52

# NEW MOON

# FULL MOON

Mercury Retrograde ends in Taurus. It brings a lucky time of thinking big about future possibilities. It is a time where you can dream big. It unlocks the right path by using creative resources and ideas. You benefit from a sense of rejuvenation, which comes from a quiet downturn. It is a time that gives you the space to nurture your dreams. If you have been feeling adrift, focusing on foundations restores equilibrium. It shifts you towards an abundant mindset and offers the chance to improve your circumstances.

As life begins to stabilize, you draw new possibilities into your social life. It highlights information arriving soon that opens a path worth growing. Life becomes brighter as greener pastures beckon. You make headway on developing a bond that offers room to further progress. It drives essential changes, and this opens to a broad vista of possibility. Small changes add up to substantial rewards over time.

Let your curiosity guide you to new endeavors. Shifting your focus away from everyday routines brings new leads and a phase of discovery. It shines a light on developing friendships and exploring social opportunities. A message reaches you, getting a chance to discuss ideas and thoughts with someone who has lately been out of the loop. It brings a sense of support and connection front and center.

The Full Moon in Sagittarius Supermoon at week's end brings a curious benefit. Expansion ahead captures the essence of freedom and creativity. Tremendous potential emerges that supports a phase of growth. It does get an auspicious chapter that supports change and advancement. It lets you take advantage of the offer that crops up as it fits into your future goals. It brings a productive chapter that connects you with a broader world of potential.

Communication is coming to your device that re-shapes your vision. It does see things picking up speed for your social life, and you thrive in this vital and dynamic environment. The conditions are right to nurture your life. It represents a new beginning that marks the start of a phase of growth that is inspired and adventurous. Waves of this potential break upon your shore as you enter a phase of developing interpersonal bonds.

You reveal a fantastic opportunity for your personal life. It comes as a surprise at first, but it gives you a glimmer of insight into the journey ahead. It does move you in alignment with your heart. Staying true to yourself draws the right situation into your life. It is a time of movement and discovery as you embrace new horizons. Exciting changes let you set sail towards a happy chapter.

Midsummer/Litha Solstice at week's end is an ideal time to reflect on your goals. An emphasis on improving circumstances draws dividends. It opens a chapter of inquiry that draws new leads and activities. In essence, it's a chance to get back to what moves your soul. Pivoting away from problematic areas brings an interest in creative endeavors. Friends, current, and new ones are coming along on this journey. It gets you in touch with pathways of support that nurture your environment.

A path of higher wisdom and learning may call your name soon. It illuminates refreshing potential that guides the way ahead. You begin to notice symbols, coincidences, and other synchronistic signs that capture your attention. A new array of options has you thinking about the possibilities. Honoring traditions and listening to inner wisdom paves the way forward.

Change swirls around your life. It brings an epiphany that opens the path ahead. It brings self-development and growth that cracks the code to wellness and harmony. The future is bright; you begin to see smooth sailing is possible even during stormy weather. Being adaptable and flexible lets, you make the most of complex environments. A new option emerges that feels like the right fit for your life. It does bring forward progress that enables you to chase a dream. Seeing your situation improve tempts you to continue to look for new leads and expand your horizons. Impressive results are available.

The New Moon in Cancer shows that it's an excellent time to review options and plot a course towards an ambitious goal. As the path clears you to reveal a new role is on offer. It lets you head full steam towards an active and vibrant phase of growth by expanding your perception and broadening the scope of your life. You discover a richly abundant path that lights a new journey forward.

You soon taste the sweet nectar of success as you unpack a chapter that focuses on nurturing your environment. It's tailor-made for cooking up dreamy plans with friends and loved ones. It has you feeling stronger, ready to take on goals with enthusiasm. It takes you on a creative journey that evolves your talents, blends ideas, and lets you come up with pathways of growth. The more you use your abilities, the brighter life becomes.

A new role is on offer. Your realistic and pragmatic approach sets the scene to achieve growth. It ramps up potential as you structure your goals in a streamlined manner. It gives you a path you can build. It brings an outstanding chapter where you achieve a rewarding outcome. Working on your life helps you notice the difference as it brings advancement to your door.

# JULY

| Sun | Mon | Tue | Wed | Thu | Fri | Sat |
|-----|-----|-----|-----|-----|-----|-----|
|     |     |     |     |     | 1   | 2   |
| 3   | 4   | 5   | 6   | 7   | 8   | 9   |
| 10  | 11  | 12  | 13  | 14  | 15  | 16  |
| 17  | 18  | 19  | 20  | 21  | 22  | 23  |
| 24  | 25  | 26  | 27  | 28  | 29  | 30  |
| 31  |     |     |     |     |     |     |

July 7th - First Quarter Moon in Libra 02:14

July 13th - Buck Moon. Full Moon in Capricorn. Supermoon 18:37

July 20th - Last Quarter Moon in Aries 14:18

July 28th - New Moon in Leo 17:54

July 28th - Delta Aquarids Meteor Shower. July 12th - August 23rd

# NEW MOON

# FULL MOON

The First Quarter Moon in Libra this week sees your social life lights up with new possibilities. It brings group involvement that connects you with like-minded individuals. You may have limiting beliefs about your ability to develop your situation. The winds of change blow into your social life; it brings a surprise or two. It has you unpacking a new chapter that heightens confidence. It rules a time of impulsivity, new adventures, and expansion. Communication cracks the code to an exciting chapter ahead.

You reveal a piece of the puzzle, and it brings insight into an area that offers room to progress your life. It helps you release doubt and anxiety; you make the right choice for your life and can embrace a grounded and balanced chapter. It does bring an environment that strengthens your life in beautiful ways.

Watch for a sign that provides an important clue; it guides you towards a new opportunity that lets you transition to a happy chapter. It does seem curious news arrives, which provides an exciting path forward. It brings inspiration flowing into your world and lets you set your sights on a lofty goal. Essential changes are arriving that bring sparkling energy; it gives you the option to improve your situation. It brings a quest of learning, growth, and self-development that takes you toward a little worn track. It gently opens the gate to an abundant path forward.

The Full Moon in Capricorn is the second Supermoon for this year. With everything changing so quickly, it can feel chaotic and unsettling. A fresh wind flows into your world, and this banishes the cobwebs. It brings new possibilities into your environment to tempt you forward. It matches you up with the unique potential of what is possible in your life, helping you remove the heaviness and embrace a more abundant landscape.

It's been difficult for you, and you needn't carry a burden on your shoulders. You may be feeling torn about heading in a new direction. Still, this transition is essential for your well-being as it does nurture your spirit. It revamps your life and focuses on leaping greener pastures. Contemplating your options provides insight into the path ahead. Gathering your resources lets you prepare to journey forward.

You ready to reveal a new path and create the life-affirming potential that begins a new chapter. It brings change; it sees you walking in a direction aligned with the person you are becoming. Expanding your vision brings options that help release the burden. It gives a sense of perspective that removes heaviness and draws healing. You have a natural knack for unveiling new potential. It's an unintuitive flair that helps create change when you need it the most—clearing your energy ushers in new possibilities. It underscores an openness to craft new goals by seeking experiences that nurture your soul.

It is a time that draws change into your life. It brings opportunities for your social life that expand your inner circle of friends. It brings an active cycle of growth that attracts the right type of people into your world. It brings liberation, freedom, and the chance to plug into your passions and create space to develop your goals. Opportunities to mingle and network put the shine on your confidence.

The more you expand your life outwardly, the more you discover the kind of experiences that support your mood. It brings the right landscape to progress your world forward. New information arrives soon that gives you a unique insight into the path ahead. It helps shed layers that hold you back, and it reveals a positive aspect that is ready to blossom under your nurturing gaze. It harnesses abilities and gives your talents a workout. It brings an excellent outlet for excess energy as it soon sees creativity overflowing.

You can expect the pace of life to pick up soon. It brings high connectivity, as people connect with you. You benefit from interacting with others, and it opens the gate to a positive and refreshing chapter. It leads to an expressive time of communication and entertaining dialogues. You spend time with those who leave you feeling valued and appreciated

A New Moon in Leo and the Delta Aquarids Meteor Shower is building new foundations on several levels. Rooting out your goals brings a breakthrough. You unearth the potential that carries you forward. Set the bar high, embrace the chapter ahead, life picks up speed as things begin to take shape. Setting aspirations and intentions to heal is the first step forward. You may be reaching for something not yet attainable and out of reach at present. Allowing a passage of time to wash away the past gently brings a phase of improving potential. You get a sense of being able to handle whatever comes along your journey of life. Your foundations improve, drawing stability, and balance into your environment. It draws harmony and heightens your confidence. It brings a time of connecting with others who offer advice and wisdom. Being involved in your social life draws an influx of potential.

Eliminating doubt expands horizons and creates space for new options to stir up creativity. You get involved with an ambitious project. It brings opportunities to explore—getting clear about the path ahead does light the way forward towards achieving more structure and stability in your life. You soon uncover a hidden gem that takes your talents further. It is a chapter that connects you to clarity. It helps you blaze a pioneering trail towards expressing your spirit, and it may well trigger a highly creative phase. There is an opportunity ahead that rejuvenates and brings new horizons into your world.

# AUGUST

| Sun | Mon | Tue | Wed | Thu | Fri | Sat |
|-----|-----|-----|-----|-----|-----|-----|
|     | 1   | 2   | 3   | 4   | 5   | 6   |
| 7   | 8   | 9   | 10  | 11  | 12  | 13  |
| 14  | 15  | 16  | 17  | 18  | 19  | 20  |
| 21  | 22  | 23  | 24  | 25  | 26  | 27  |
| 28  | 29  | 30  | 31  |     |     |     |

# ASTROLOGY

August 5th - First Quarter Moon Scorpio 11:06

August 8th - Full Moon in Aquarius Supermoon 01:35. Sturgeon Moon.

August 8th - Perseids Meteor Shower July 17th - August 24th

August 14th - Saturn at Opposition

August 19th - Last Quarter Moon in Taurus 04:36

August 27th - New Moon in Virgo 08:16

August 27th - Mercury at Greatest Eastern Elongation at 27.3 degrees from the Sun

# NEW MOON

# FULL MOON

You may find the pace of your life settling down. One positive aspect of this time is it increases the stability that grounds your foundation as it balances your environment. It begins a positive trend that offers renewal and relaxation. It does bring a chance to use technology to an advantage to stay connected with friends and your social circle. The work you do behind-the-scenes is instrumental in connecting the dots of a new chapter. It ushers in change and brings a social aspect that becomes a focus for you moving forward.

Your efforts to improve your circumstances bear fruit when you discover a new growth pathway. Life picks up steam, and this brings a new vista that brings the development of skills. It unleashes your talents and an area ripe for expansion. Advancement is in the pipeline, and it lets you go at a comfortable pace, which improves balance.

You may be hesitating and uncertain about the path ahead. Something new and inspiring is ready to happen for you soon. It brings a change to your routine and opens a gateway forward. It does signify a turning point that helps you discover a path of inspiration. Setting intentions and staying positive helps pave the way towards an enterprising chapter of developing goals. It lets you build dreams sustainably and create firm foundations that offer security. There is a lot of newness coming bringing options to dabble in a creative undertaking.

Full Moon in Aquarius Supermoon and the Perseids Meteor Shower this week sees essential changes that bring a leap of faith. It is a time that draws options that encourage you to expand your life and explore your world's potential. Things are on the move for you soon. It brings unscripted adventures and a chance to mingle with friends. It lets you branch out and explore new options. A progressive phase of social engagement draws abundance, security, and good fortune. It sweeps in a direction that lifts your spirits. It lets you chart a course towards a happier chapter. It inspires creativity and fans the flames of your inspiration.

The future is looking rosy as it brings new options. Indeed, you are currently on the cusp of change; information arrives, bringing a curious shift forward. It kicks off a unique phase of expansion that cultivates the right conditions to develop your social life. People and potential come into your life and rock your world. It sets the stage for a lively journey that brings new friends and companions. The emphasis is on improving home life and security. You can remove the barriers and open the door to a new chapter. It brings lighter energy that brings a boost. It is a time of growing your confidence, which sets the stage to expand your social life. You are on a journey towards a brighter future, and as you make this passage forward, people enter into your life to tempt you in a new direction. It fuels options for a broader social circle. Lively discussions and heightened communication ensure you are kept busy.

Hidden information makes itself known that brings the confidence to strike out in a new area. It connects you with others who support and value your contribution— movement, discovery, and inspiration weave pure magic. Prioritizing your needs opens a path of wellness and rejuvenation. It has a profound effect on improving your circumstances.

A new possibility crops up that eases your troubles. It often is a chapter of harmony that draws happiness as it opens the door to a fresh start. It does let you ride out the turbulence and enter smoother waters. A situation you invest your energy into developing blossoms into a journey worth progressing. It helps you branch out and explore uncharted territory.

New possibilities emerge this week that spark improvement. Cultivating the potential possible draws an energizing chapter. It is a pivotal time for advancing your life forward. An area you get involved with holds promise. It defines the path ahead and connects you with kindred spirits. It brings a creative collaboration that gets you engaged with working with a joint project. It gives you a chance to catch up with friends, and this harmonizes your foundations. Opening the shutters lets the magic blossom in your world.

In Virgo this week, New Moon combined with Mercury at Greatest Eastern Elongation from the Sun to heighten potential. There is an emphasis on advancing your life. You diligently lay the groundwork, and this takes you closer to your goals. It connects you with a journey of personal growth that propels you forward. It does bring signs and luck into your life. Life-affirming possibilities connect you with kindred spirits who are on a similar trajectory. Linking up with a tribe of like-minded individuals takes you towards an active environment that improves your world. Challenges ahead offer a chance to lean into discomfort and grow your abilities by pushing back barriers that limit potential.

Making tracks towards your vision, you enter an enterprising chapter that brings options. It lets you land in an environment that is ripe for progression. New responsibilities may add an extra layer of complexity. Still, you're up to the challenge as it takes you where you need to go. Feeling the heat grows your abilities. It lets you navigate a complicated phase and come out a winner. Branching out brings a boost.

Paying attention to signs and synchronicity links you up to a chapter that offers room to improve your world. Your journey is evolving, and as sunny skies emerge overhead, you step out and enjoy developing a new chapter. News arrives that lights a path forward; it gives you the green light to move onto your next big project.

# SEPTEMBER

| Sun | Mon | Tue | Wed | Thu | Fri | Sat |
|-----|-----|-----|-----|-----|-----|-----|
|     |     |     |     | 1   | 2   | 3   |
| 4   | 5   | 6   | 7   | 8   | 9   | 10  |
| 11  | 12  | 13  | 14  | 15  | 16  | 17  |
| 18  | 19  | 20  | 21  | 22  | 23  | 24  |
| 25  | 26  | 27  | 28  | 29  | 30  |     |

September 7th - First Quarter Moon Sagittarius 18:08

September 10th - Mercury Retrograde begins in Libra

September 10th - Corn Moon. Harvest Moon. Full Moon in Pisces 09:58

September 16th - Neptune at Opposition

September 17th - Last Quarter Moon in Gemini 21:52

September 23 - Mabon/Fall Equinox. 01:03

September 25th - New Moon in Libra 21:54

September 26th - Jupiter at Opposition

# NEW MOON

# FULL MOON

News is imminent; it provides a new option. The wheels are in motion to move away from situations that limit your potential. It is a time of growth that brings insight into pathways forward. It offers room to grow your social life; you are on the right track towards improving your circumstances. Connecting with a broader range of people brings the chance to nurture friendships and draw enrichment into your social life. It does see you spending more time with friends and companions. Lively discussions bring new thoughts and ideas to light. Being expressive about what you seek helps you chart a course towards your chosen destination. It does get a time that draws new people into your world.

Someone in your broader community is holding a big secret around you. The next time you bump into this person, they reveal a desire to chat and mingle with you. It seems they have a special message to share and hope to get the ball rolling to develop a closer bond. An adventure beckons that draws improvements and harmony. There is a focus on deepening a bond and exploring the potential with a new companion. It initiates a positive trend for your social life that has you feeling excited and inspired. It sparks conversations that nurture well-being. The changes ahead keep you involved and on your toes. It is a busy and active time that expands your social life. It does shine a light on nurturing a friendship along.

Mercury Retrograde begins in Libra. Harvest Moon. Full Moon in Pisces If you feel weighed down at this time, remember communication and activities are available to nourish your soul. Don't completely close the door on your social life during a Mercury retrograde phase; remember to stay involved and connected with others. A person is working behind the scenes, which brings support to your door soon.

It is a highly compatible time for nurturing creativity. It does bring projects and endeavors to keep you busy. Immersing yourself in a creative interest balances your foundations. It captures your attention and keeps you focused on using your talents, spending time on activities that bring wellness and abundance into your world. News arrives that brings a surprise. An impromptu get-together brings lively discussions and a chance to blend ideas. It is the remedy to the sense of restriction that has clung to your energy recently. It lifts the lid on a new chapter that sparkles with possibility.

Indeed, your perseverance and patience provide a smoother journey soon. The new potential is brewing in the background of your life. Information arrives that shines a light on a refreshing chapter. It lets you move forward with your social life once again. It opens the gateway towards a happy environment that connects you with friends.

You have been putting on a brave face during a difficult chapter. Answering the more essential questions that swirl around your life takes you to a crossroads. You make a decision that opens the floodgates, and this lets you embrace a happier chapter. It transitions towards a social time of exploring new options and connecting with friends and companions. Inspiration and creativity heighten, and this helps you come up with innovative solutions. There is a focus on emotional wellness, which centers your attention on developing interpersonal bonds that hold water. Removing the drama and setting barriers set the bar higher for your personal life.

You can release your troubles and doubts. Removing the stress and tension brings a turning point. It allows complications to fade away, and this brings sunny skies overhead. Your perseverance and patience draw dividends. It brings stability and consistency to your life. You become immersed in developing an area that blossoms under your nurturing touch. It has you exploring new pathways of growth and engaging in activities that nurture your spirit. A gathering of friends brings lively discussions; it gets the ball rolling on an inspiring social connection chapter. A shift is occurring that brings fundamental changes to your social life. It does see certain friendships drifting away when a new flow of potential connects you with opportunities to mingle. It grows a journey that offers unique experiences and friendships. More security is on offer, which creates a stable platform.

Mabon/Fall Equinox. New Moon in Libra. Jupiter at Opposition. It brings the chance to reboot and rejuvenate your life from the ground up. You unpack a colorful chapter that brings new possibilities. It lets you contribute your energy towards developing an area of interest. It does heighten creativity and sees inspiration return full force. It brings the perfect environment to collaborate and connect with others who have similar goals. Unique opportunities ahead take you towards expansion and freedom.

The more you work on your vision, the better the chances are for advancing your goals. It brings structure and stability, taking your skills to a new level. Working with technology sees you working smarter and joining forces with kindred spirits. It brings positive change that improves the day-to-day running of your life.

The trials of the past have tested you on many levels. As you take tentative steps forward, you see promising signs that your fortune is ready to turn a corner and head to a brighter chapter. A lucky break arrives that paves the way for a harmonious phase of progressing goals. It blends innovation with practical aspects; it draws a winning combination that improves stability. You get involved with developing skills and nurture an area that shows promise.

# OCTOBER

| Sun | Mon | Tue | Wed | Thu | Fri | Sat |
|-----|-----|-----|-----|-----|-----|-----|
|     |     |     |     |     |     | 1   |
| 2   | 3   | 4   | 5   | 6   | 7   | 8   |
| 9   | 10  | 11  | 12  | 13  | 14  | 15  |
| 16  | 17  | 18  | 19  | 20  | 21  | 22  |
| 23  | 24  | 25  | 26  | 27  | 28  | 29  |
| 30  | 31  |     |     |     |     |     |

# ASTROLOGY

October 2nd - Mercury Retrograde ends in Virgo

October 3rd - First Quarter Moon in Capricorn 00.14

October 7th - Draconids Meteor Shower. Oct 6th-10th

October 8th - Mercury Greatest Western Elongation

October 9th - Hunters Moon. Full Moon in Aries 20:54

October 17th - Last Quarter Moon in Cancer 17.15

October 21st -Orionids Meteor Shower. October 2nd - November 7th

October 25th - New Moon in Scorpio 10:48

October 25th - Partial Solar Eclipse

# NEW MOON

# FULL MOON

Mercury Retrograde ends, and your life holds a change that brings social engagement. A transformational aspect lets you put your best foot forward. The more deeply you delve into your future vision, the greater the freedom that surrounds your life. It enables you to move beyond limitation towards the discovery of new pathways that encourage growth. Connecting with a broader social environment paves the way forward.

It is a pivotal time where you create positive change. It brings a vibrant landscape that places a focus on expansion. Your social life brings incoming opportunities to network and mingle. It puts you in the right zone to connect with friends and companions. It provides insightful communication while promoting harmony and support. Sharing thoughts and ideas draw a trailblazing path forward. It becomes a focal point as you move forward as you connect with someone inspiring. It brings a time of chasing dreams and following your heart.

Enchanting information arrives that promotes harmony and wellness. It lights a new path forward for your social life. Your willingness to unearth new options see greener pastures beckon. A flood of exciting possibilities is ready to be explored. It takes you towards growth and expansion. Life becomes brighter; you open the door to a carefree journey that lets you set sail on your ship of dreams.

The Full Moon in Aries elevates potential this week. Events on the horizon trigger a time that grows the path ahead. It gets you involved with breaking down limitations and finding workarounds that connect you with your social life. It increases the sense of security as it draws well-being and harmony. It dissolves boundaries, and let's opportunity come knocking. It does see the sharing of thoughts and ideas with someone attentive and thoughtful.

You may be feeling like you're on an emotional rollercoaster. You can ride out the turbulence and make remarkable progress. Life brings adventure and harmony to your world. A new option arrives soon that leaves you feeling energized and excited. It sparks beautiful changes that attract the type of possibilities that offer growth and stability. It charts a journey towards a promising phase of luck and prosperity. A focus on self-development and creativity provides pathways forward. A leap of faith expands horizons into unique areas. Things work out for the best. It brings a whirlwind of activity and sharing thoughts and ideas with others who understand. It lets you explore a passage forward, and it shows the marked improvement of stability. Seeds planted during this chapter ripen and blossom over the coming months.

You can stay open to new resources and pathways that draw a sense of connection and support. Life sparks with fresh inspiration that marks new beginnings. It brings a phase of growth and learning that develops an area of interest. You can make strides towards improving your circumstances and build foundations that draw stability into your world.

New pathways are ready to open. Events line up to provide an extraordinary window of opportunity. It takes you towards a supportive time that focuses on sharing thoughts and communication with another. The energy of abundance resonates throughout this time. You connect with someone who has a strong sense of integrity. From the get-go, they are proactive, supportive, and endearing.

It brings the right balance in your life that blesses your world with increasing harmony. You ground yourself in the basics; getting back to the building blocks of life lets you fully appreciate the potential ahead. It shines a light on a path of well-being and happiness. You plant the seeds of your dreams in fertile soil, and they blossom into an abundant tree of life. Your gifts of empathy and compassion foster a connection that draws meaning into your world.

.

The New Moon in Scorpio sees you lift the lid on an enterprising chapter that brings exciting developments. A new source of prosperity flows into your world and draws stability. It offers a blueprint for future growth. Choices and decisions ahead trigger a path of growth and advancement. It helps you move away from issues that drain energy and disrupt your focus. Navigating between developing your life and creating space to nurture your creativity draws balance.

A new area calls your name soon. If you have found things have slowed down, it does catch your eye and connect you with a journey worth growing. The more you improve your circumstances, the greater the chances are that new potential will flow into your world as a tributary flows into the ocean. Your willingness to explore options plays an essential part in bringing success to your door. Plotting future goals gets the ball rolling and does set a powerful intention that it's going to happen. You are doing the right thing by keeping open to change, and a lead is found that takes you where you need to be next. You test the water and it marks the beginning of a significant transition that nurtures your talents and grows your abilities. It brings the chance to connect with others who desire to collaborate on joint projects and endeavors

# NOVEMBER

| Sun | Mon | Tue | Wed | Thu | Fri | Sat |
|-----|-----|-----|-----|-----|-----|-----|
|     |     | 1   | 2   | 3   | 4   | 5   |
| 6   | 7   | 8   | 9   | 10  | 11  | 12  |
| 13  | 14  | 15  | 16  | 17  | 18  | 19  |
| 20  | 21  | 22  | 23  | 24  | 25  | 26  |
| 27  | 28  | 29  | 30  |     |     |     |

November 1st - First Quarter Moon in Aquarius 06.37

November 4th - Taurids Meteor Shower. September 7th - December 10th

November 8th - Full Moon in Taurus 11:01 Beaver Moon. November 8th - Total Lunar Eclipse

November 9th - Uranus at Opposition

November 16th - Last Quarter Moon in Leo 13:27

November 17th - Leonids Meteor Shower Nov 6th-30th

November 23rd - New Moon in Sagittarius 22:57

November 30th - First Quarter Moon Pisces 14:36

# NEW MOON

# FULL MOON

The Taurids Meteor rains blessings on your world this week. Nurturing your foundations brings rewards; it creates space to develop talents. It awakens you to the potential possible in your world. Heading back to basics brings an original and unique journey that offers room to grow your abilities into new areas. Change ahead brings a theme of improving circumstances. New possibilities emerge with a flourish, and this clears the path ahead. It brings rapid change that can feel unsettling, but it also encourages growth. You plant the seeds that blossom into an enterprising path forward towards your chosen destination.

It does allow you to open a new chapter forward with purposefulness. A resolution to direct your energy towards developing your life draws dividends. You can create space to explore the new potential. A critical decision unlocks a chapter of growth. Exciting changes are ready to sweep into your world.

It is a time of growing your world, and it brings a new approach. It leads to a time filled with magic and mayhem. It gets a chance to use your grit and determination to overcome hurdles and reach your destination. As you improve your foundations, you branch out and develop other areas of life. It creates a ripple effect that sees benefits flowing into your world. A pleasant surprise lands in your lap soon.

The Full Moon in Taurus combines with a Total Lunar Eclipse. It does create space to progress your life. Developing your dreams, moving your life in alignment with emotional awareness brings meaning. It sets the right foundations from which to grow your world. It connects you with others who hold similar values, and this favors growth for your social life. It is the richly creative process that is at the crux of this energy. Information arrives that inspires change soon.

It draws an enriching time that brings inner happiness and fulfillment. It does draw creative pursuits that help you put the finishing touches on your new life. It bodes well for your circumstances and sets the tone for a refreshing change that brings a welcome sense of freedom and expansion.

If you pivot in a new direction, it does draw new options. You reveal information that brings insight into developing a new area. It brings change and a dynamic environment for setting goals. It does let you plot a course towards advancing your abilities. An active phase of growth and development tap into a busy time that nurtures your talents. Your ability to develop your vision grows by leaps and bounds.

Leonids Meteor Shower brings a landmark moment, and it is a gateway toward a brighter future. Expanding your reach into new areas draws dividends. It brings lightness to your life as you thing see things lining up. It offers a journey of growth and prosperity. A revelation stirs the energy of manifestation, and it has you thinking big about the possibilities. A luminescent path glitters with new gems. Growth and progression move you forward. Indeed, opening the way ahead brings a blossoming chapter.

Information arrives that captures your attention. The path ahead shines with a new possibility, and it is a sweet gift after all the uncertainty. Your prospects brightly burn as something is on offer that helps you scope out a new field of potential. It gives you the option to go ahead with following a course that seems like the right fit. Getting involved with this environment draws an enriching chapter.

As circumstances shift and change, you open up pathways that serve your soul well. It draws a time of relaxation and rejuvenation. An emphasis on improving your circumstances lights a progressive path that offers a wellspring of abundance. It brings a journey that provides room to tackle a long-held dream. You plant seeds of inspiration in fertile ground, and this brings a winning option into focus. An opportunity ahead helps your quest to develop this goal; it ushers in an engaging atmosphere.

New Moon in Sagittarius You enter an energizing time that hits a high note. It opens a path that reveals new information. Lovely changes are ready to flow into your world. It highlights choice, expansion, and change. It brings an environment that is soul-affirming and emotionally rewarding. New energy blossoms and this is a breath of fresh air. It brings a friendly and relaxing chapter that brings opportunities to mingle. It does renew and rejuvenate; it lets you turn the page on a fresh chapter in your book of life.

It connects you with a path that grows your abilities. Expanding into new areas leaves you feeling energized. It does bring excitement as you gain traction on a larger vision of what is possible. You enjoy a favorable chapter that brings new pathways to contemplate. Directing your energy on expanding your life, outwardly draws dividends. It brings a rosy time that correlates with learning and growth.

It brings a sense of excitement and a feeling that life is lining up beautifully for you when an impromptu get-together draws engaging conversations. You discover a clear path opens, and this brings an exciting possibility into your personal life. It speaks of the journey that draws meaning and abundance. Instead of worrying about the destination, you embrace the trip and all that it entails.

# DECEMBER

| Sun | Mon | Tue | Wed | Thu | Fri | Sat |
|-----|-----|-----|-----|-----|-----|-----|
|     |     |     |     | 1   | 2   | 3   |
| 4   | 5   | 6   | 7   | 8   | 9   | 10  |
| 11  | 12  | 13  | 14  | 15  | 16  | 17  |
| 18  | 19  | 20  | 21  | 22  | 23  | 24  |
| 25  | 26  | 27  | 28  | 29  | 30  | 31  |

December 8th - Cold Moon. Moon Before Yule
December 8th - Full Moon in Gemini 04:07
December 8th - Mars at Opposition

December 13th - Geminids Meteor Shower. Dec 7th - 17th

December 16th - Last Quarter Moon in Virgo 08:56

December 21st - Ursids Meteor Shower December 17 - 25th December 21 - Mercury at Greatest Eastern elongation.
December 21st - Yule/Winter Solstice at 09:48

December 23rd - New Moon in Capricorn 10:16

December 29th - Mercury Retrograde begins in Capricorn

December 30th - First Quarter Moon Aries 01:21

# NEW MOON

# FULL MOON

You have a secret admirer who watches from afar. This person has been watching and waiting for a chance to get to know you better. It does draw a sweet chapter filled with lively conversations. Connecting with this person brings a heightened sense of confidence and well-being. You enter a landscape filled with potential, your willingness to be open to new environments and situations is instrumental in bringing the goodness up to the surface. It does open the path ahead and offer a chance to advance your social life.

You reveal information that charms and inspires. It lets you make headway on expanding your social life. It brings an adventure-driven chapter that moves you out of your comfort zone and lets you mingle. It does seem that change is surrounding your environment; someone seeks to become closer. It does light a path towards abundance. Following your intuition is the ticket to success with this individual. This person is a sensitive soul and plays a pivotal role in developing your personal life.

Flashes of insight and creativity spark growth. Hedging your bets lets you make an informed choice before setting off on a new adventure. A sense of wanderlust captures the essence of magic and adventure. It does have you dreaming big and focusing on an enterprising avenue. An area you nurture takes on a life of its own and brings an active growth and expansion phase.

Full Moon in Gemini with Mars at Opposition shows that you are undergoing a transition that may feel jarring but keep focusing on advancing your life. It does help you discover the diamond in the rough, and this unearths a journey of glittering possibility. It encourages you to diverge from the safe and known and embrace exploring new potential. It lights up pathways of creativity and expression. It is a chance to develop your life and widen the scope of potential in your world. A great deal of excitement is ahead, and this is the sweet taste of success.

While things may feel up in the air, you soon land in a settled environment that connects you with friends, colleagues, and kindred spirits. It lets you embrace a social aspect that matches up the potential with new possibilities. A chance encounter brings an invitation, and this gives you a chance to mingle with a friend who seeks to become closer. It does resonate with abundance and draws well-being. You can maintain good bonds and develop friendships by thinking out of the box and implementing new strategies.

An emphasis on improving your circumstances influences the energy coming into your life. It brings options that encourage growth and expansion. It does heighten a sense of self-worth and confidence that lets you expand barriers and move out of your usual comfort zone.

Ursids Meteor Shower. Mercury at Greatest Eastern elongation. Yule/Winter Solstice at week's end. It is a carefree and happy festive season. You can relax and let your guard down in a social environment. A new cycle is ready to begin; it brings friends and companions that offer joy and support. It underscores a theme of rejuvenation and evolution swirling around your environment. New possibilities flow into your world and spark your inspiration. A creative undertaking garners terrific recognition.

It is a curious time; it offers a chance to develop your social life. Using technology to your advantage opens pathways to connect with others of a similar mindset. Good luck flows into your life when a communication arrives that bestows blessings on your world. It advances your vision, and life becomes more connected and abundant. Moving out of your comfort zone, you get a sense of the kind of growth that is possible.

There are changes ahead that bring a turning point. It liberates you from worry and translates to an exceptional time that draws abundance and social engagement. It brings the security you seek; it helps you forge social connections that are stable and secure. It triggers a new chapter for your home life that draws blessings into your world.

New Moon in Capricorn this week speaks of a social aspect that brings you an advantage. It offers an opportunity to socialize, expanding your life outwardly, you explore a new realm of possibilities. It does bring opportunities to mingle and connect with friends and companions. A unique area of interest. It promotes harmony and offers renewal and relaxation. The wind carries news that expands your vision.

News arrives that brings a new direction. It rules a chapter of expansion and adventure. An active and dynamic environment fires up ambitions and takes you to a new topic of interest. It draws an essential time for advancing goals and developing abilities. Improving your skills nurtures a strong foundation from which to grow your life. Exploring options lets, you plot a proper course forward.

Exciting opportunities are ready to roll into your world. It connects you to a social aspect that brings the chance to network and mingle. It is a vivid and dynamic flowing chapter that brings friends and companions together. A wellspring of abundance flows into your life: support and the feeling of connection with others. It sparks a lively and social time that brings a thoughtful path to explore.

Dear Stargazer,

I hope you have enjoyed planning your year with the stars utilizing Astrology and Zodiac influences. My yearly zodiac books feature a weekly (four weeks to a month) horoscope. You can find me on this website, where you can get personal astrology or intuitive readings.

https://psychic-emails.com/


Follow me on social media here:

https://www.facebook.com/SiaSands

Instagram: SiaSands


Leaving a review for my book is welcomed and appreciated.


Many Blessings,

Sia Sands

Made in the USA
Middletown, DE
30 November 2021

53836505R00068